The **beloved community** is not a utopia, but a place
where the barriers between people gradually come down
and where the citizens make a constant effort to address
even the most difficult problems of ordinary people.
It is above all else an idealistic community.

— Reverend Jim Lawson

Rev. James Lawson, born in Pennsylvania in 1928, grew up in Ohio where he spoke out early in his life against war and racial injustice. Called the "teacher of the civil rights movement" by the Rev. Jesse Jackson, Rev. Lawson often talked about the concept of "the beloved community." His life has been dedicated to serving his fellow man and working for justice. Currently he serves as pastor emeritus of the Holman United Methodist Church in Los Angeles where he continues to work with community organizations and interfaith coalitions.

acknowledgements

There are a hundred or more people who will say, "I am part of that story" when they read this book. There is no way to rightly thank one person for the contribution he or she makes to another person's life. This is sacred. We can thank one another for the gift of community. We hope that you, as a reader, find a way to join in and be part of the journey.

We can thank Ashley O'Brien, Connie Lyle O'Brien, John O'Brien, Jack Pearpoint, Michelle Karner and Linda Wittish for helping us bring this story to you. Thanks also to these Savannahians for their support in the publication of this book: Sheldon and Zelda Tenenbaum, Howard and Mary Morrison, Joe and Carol Bell, Connor's Temple Baptist Church, Philip and Cathy Solomons and Bill and Gigi Haile.

Cover Credit: The front cover is two pages of Mrs. Addie Reeves' hand made telephone and address book. Each letter was individually cut from a church bulletin or newspaper and glued into the book over roughly a 25 year period. See and read more on page 75.

MARSHA FOREST (1942-2000) INSPIRED OTHERS WITH HER PASSIONATE AND UNCOMPROMISING ADVOCACY FOR INCLUSION. A MARSHA FOREST BOOK COMMUNICATES IN HER SPIRIT.

Preparation of this publication was partially supported through a subcontract to Responsive System Associates from the Center on Human Policy, Syracuse University for the Research and Training Center on Community Living. The Research and Training Center on Community Living is supported through a cooperative agreement (number H133B031116) between the National Institute on Disability & Rehabilitation Research (NIDRR) and the University of Minnesota Institute on Community Integration. Members of the Center are encouraged to express their opinions; these do not necessarily represent the official position of NIDRR.

Book designed by Michelle Karner.

Library and Archives Canada Cataloguing in Publication

Kohler, Tom
Waddie Welcome and the beloved community/ Tom Kohler and Susan Earl.

Includes bibliological references and index.
ISBN 1-895418-54-2

1. Welcome, Waddie. 2. Social integration--Georgia--Savannah.
3. People with disabilities--Deinstitutionalization--Georgia--Savannah.
4. Social advocacy--Georgia--Savannah. I. Earl, Susan II. Title

HV3020.2.U52S28 2004   362.4'048   C2004-905209-8

© 2004 by Inclusion Press; 2010 Second Printing; 2012 Third Printing

Printed in Canada by Couto Printing and Publishing Services

Inclusion Press
47 Indian Trail • Toronto • Ontario • Canada • M6R 1Z8
Tel: 416-658-5363   Fax: 416-658-5067
E-mail: inclusionpress@inclusion.com

www.inclusion.com

contents

introduction

from the authors

Our purpose is to tell a story about a man named Waddie Welcome. This telling of Mr. Welcome's story began as I joined slides and written materials along with a reflection written by Susan Earl, to create a talk for people concerned with community building as done by people associated with Chatham Savannah Citizen Advocacy. Response to the talk and slide show led to this book.

We are telling the story as we understand it. We do not know all of it. Much of it took place before our time and much of it happened without us present. A lot of this story comes from other people's stories.

We would not usually be telling another person's story in such detail; people's lives are private. But in the latter part of his life, Mr. Welcome became a public figure and a man who felt his life had a message. Mr. Welcome's great nieces have seen the story and consider it to be respectful.

what is citizen advocacy?

A valued citizen, who is unpaid and independent of human services, creates a relationship with a person who is at risk of social exclusion. The citizen advocate chooses one or several of many ways to understand, respond to and represent that person's interests as if they were the advocate's own. Over time, the advocate looks for ways to bring his protege's gifts and concerns into the circle of ordinary community life.

Citizen advocacy is heart-warming and heart-wrenching. It is unpredictable, which is both a strength and a weakness. In citizen advocacy language, this is the story of one match — the match between Mr. Waddie Welcome and Mr. Lester Johnson. Tom Kohler met Waddie Welcome and asked Lester Johnson to become Mr. Welcome's citizen advocate.

A mantra in citizen advocacy is "more people, more people, more people" — bring more good people into the life of a person who is excluded from relationship and community life. A citizen advocacy coordinator will sometimes help a citizen advocate build a constituency of allies to broaden and sustain action on behalf of his or her protege. This is one such story.

foreword

When I look at the photographs of Waddie Welcome in this book and see that great grin, I respond in kind. What a legacy! But then — to read the story — the legacy expands into life lessons for us all. Waddie Welcome's life gives new meaning to the phrase "power to the people." Power is an intriguing concept, and this story opens up for exploration the power of personal story, the power of personal relationships, the power of prayer, the power of place, the power of persistence and the power of the possible.

When I was in the civil rights movement of the '60s, the beloved community meant an unspoken acceptance of anyone who believed in and was willing to work for human rights, dignity, justice and equality for every person. Waddie Welcome and his allies literally built a beloved community from within their community in Savannah, Georgia. Now, more than ever, we need to see each person — each other — as indeed "beloved," and to follow Waddie Welcome's example and build a broader, deeper, beloved community, knowing that Mr. Welcome is smiling at us still and always.

— Connie Curry

Author and activist Connie Curry was a founding member of the Student Non-violent Coordinating Committee (SNCC) and later was the Southern field representative of the American Friends Service Committee. In recent years, she has explored the unfinished business of the 1960s through books ("Silver Rights," "The Fire Ever Burning," "Deep in Our Hearts: Nine White Women in the Freedom Movement," and "Mississippi Harmony"). She lives in Atlanta.

Born on the 4th of July

— Tom Kohler

This is the house where Mr. Welcome grew up. The porch is important. Carrie Welcome, Waddie's mother, had a treats store with cookies, candy and pickles for sale. Mr. Welcome was always ready to help her. His job was to alert his mother if anyone came and violated the money jar's honor system.

Waddie Welcome was born July 4, 1914, in Sylvania, Georgia. He was one of five brothers and two sisters. His mother and father, Carrie and Henry Welcome, moved to Savannah, Georgia in the mid-1920s. They most likely came to town in a wooden mule-drawn wagon. They settled on Battery Street in the Cuyler community, which is just southwest of downtown Savannah.

Today this area would be considered the interior of the city with several miles of residential and commercial development surrounding it. In Waddie Welcome's early days, this neighborhood would have been much more rural, with lots of large gardens, plenty of chicken coops and more than a few milk cows. Outhouses would have been used, and were, in fact, used until the 1920s when the city fathers were forced largely by their wives and their own gastronomical self-interests to put in the infrastructure for standard plumbing.*

Mr. Welcome lived with his family for more than 70 years. He saw his brothers and sisters grow up and go, leaving the repressive South for more opportunity in other parts of the country. He saw his mother and father age. After his parents died, Mr. Welcome's brother, Willie Welcome, took care of him for several years. Adult Protective Services placed Waddie in a nursing home after neighbors expressed concern about his care not being adequate.

* Rev. John Q. Adams, one of Savannah's oldest teachers and ministers, described how the fear of tuberculosis being brought into the kitchens of influential Savannahians' homes by their black maids and cooks who lived in Cuyler-Brownville, helped force public expenditure for modern sanitation in the neighborhood. (Private conversation between John Q. Adams and a small group of Savannahians who formed an Indigenous Wisdom Listening Circle in the mid-1980s.)

In the 1920s, '30s, '40s, '50s and '60s the neighborhood was more prominent, more middle class. During these years, many people emerged as community and national leaders in their fields. In the '70s '80s and '90s, the neighborhood began to get rougher, with more absentee landlords. Juanitia's, shown above, is located at 703 1/2 W. 37th St.

The Savannah Checker Club, located on the corner of Burroughs and 39th St., is in Mr. Welcome's neighborhood. It costs $1 a month to be a member.

SUSAN EARL

ANN CURRY

ANN CURRY

Mr. Welcome's neighborhood, like most urban neighborhoods, had a very distinct daytime and nighttime life. Mr. Welcome preferred untaxed spirits to taxed spirits. He loved to be in the company of men huddled together — drinking, talking, laughing. Sharon's Lounge, shown above, is located at 618 Montgomery St.

Connor's Temple Baptist Church sits on the southwest corner of the neighborhood. Mr. and Mrs. Welcome and all of their children were members. Henry Welcome was a deacon and even though he was blind for a good part of his adult life, he taught Sunday School. He committed long portions of the Bible to memory.

Annual Spring Revival

Jerusalem Baptist Church
Rev. J. Hardy, Pastor

Guest Speaker
Rev. Franklin Taylor, Pastor
Don Tabernacle Baptist Church
Jackson Park Baptist Church
MAY 21, 22, 23   7:30 P.M.

SUSAN EARL

This is not a corporate neighborhood, but a neighborhood where people use what they have. There is a feel of hands-on resourcefulness to it.

The neighborhood is dotted with churches of all types. Jerusalem Baptist Church, shown here, is located at 635 W. 41st St. and was likely hand-built by the membership.

Second Bethlehem Baptist Church is located at 615 Montgomery St., just to the east of the neighborhood. Church dinners are cooked and served daily — good food: red rice, chitterlings, collards.

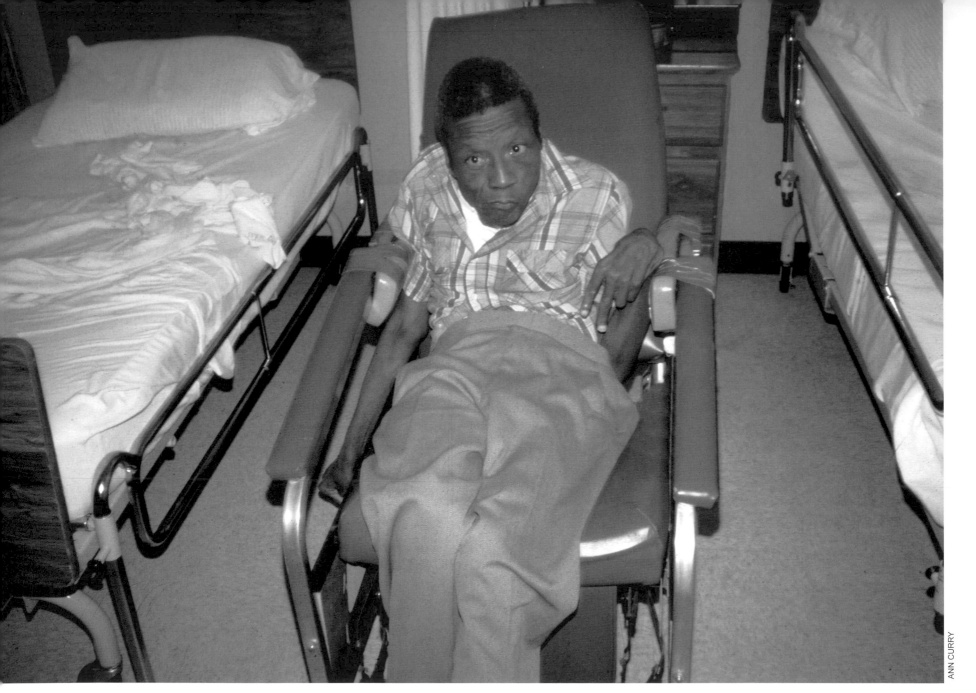

Waddie Welcome in the mid-1980s at Savannah Health Care Nursing Home on White Bluff Road.

I met Mr. Welcome in 1986 as he was reclining in what is called an adult high chair in the hallway of Savannah Health Care Nursing Home. I pushed his chair back into his room, closed the door for privacy and bent down to start talking with him. As I spoke, he would listen and try to respond, but then he would look over my left shoulder. I would speak again, trying to get and hold his attention. Again he would try and push words out of his mouth and then start staring over my shoulder. I repositioned myself a little closer to be more prominent in his view, but after speaking to him for a few moments, he again gazed over my shoulder. Finally I turned around and saw that Mr. Welcome was looking at a California cruising poster — the one with three young women in string bikinis standing in the bed of a tricked-up pick-up truck. Let's just say the photo was not taken from the front of the truck. Well, I swung back around to look at Mr. Welcome, and he cracked up laughing. And that's really when I began to learn something about who this man was. This was a man with a sharp and never tiring eye for the ladies. In the South, if the man is an older man not a younger man, we call that man a cooter.

I tried to recruit a citizen advocate for Mr. Welcome, and it took a long time. I asked 39 people. No one said yes.

During that time, the state of Georgia closed Savannah Health Care Nursing Home because of health and safety violations. Mr. Welcome was social worked out of Savannah to a nursing home in Abbeyville, Georgia, three hours due west by car. I found and visited Mr. Welcome. I asked if he wanted to come back to Savannah. Every muscle in his body screamed, "Yes!"

Southside Nursing Facility Has Medicaid Payments Cut

By TOM BARTON
Staff Writer

State Medicaid officials said Wednesday they have cut off reimbursements for any new residents admitted to a southside nursing home, pending the outcome of a recent inspection at the facility.

Inspectors informed Savannah Health Care Nursing Home at 12825 White Bluff Road in a Sept. 20 letter that the facility "was not meeting standards" for care, said Aaron Johnson, commissioner of the Georgia Department of Medical Assistance.

Last week, inspectors made a follow-up visit at the nursing home to see if the problems had been corrected, Johnson said. A final report is expected in a few days.

"We are denying (Medicaid) payment for any new admissions," Johnson said.

The denial of payment is standard procedure in such cases, he said.

If the problems have been corrected, Medicaid reimbursements for new residents would resume. If deficiencies remain, however, the state could cut off reimbursements for all residents whose nursing home stays are covered by Medicaid, Johnson said.

Wesley Vincent, administrator of the three-year-old, 120-bed nursing home said Wednesday that 12 licensed practical nurses employed at the facility have been fired for "gross medication errors" in caring for residents.

Those errors included not giving residents their medicines according to doctors' orders and incorrectly recording the times such medicines were administered, Vincent said.

"The conditions caused by the nurses could be dangerous to patients' lives. We were severely reprimanded for it," Vincent said.

The nursing home has since hired 12 new LPNs to help treat the 100 residents there, he said.

SUSAN EARL

Mrs. Addie Reeves

I found a letter in Mr. Welcome's nightstand. It was addressed in pencil — a big, fat, #2 Clark lead pencil — and the return address said A. Reeves, 115 Walz Street, Savannah, Georgia.

I got back to Savannah and called directory assistance and found a phone number for Addie Reeves and called. After some abstract yammering on my part, she said, "Is this about Waddie?" I said "Yes," and she said, "Come on over!" I said, "I'd like to set up an appointment to come visit next week." And she said, "Come on over!" I said, "I'd like to come next week," and she said, "Is this about Waddie Welcome?" and I said "Yes" and mumbled something about wanting to arrange an appointment. Thirty minutes later I was standing on the doorstep of 115 Walz Street in Yamacraw Village.

Now I am not proud of this, but I'm just gonna say it. When I was growing up, "Yamacraw" was used by a lot of people I grew up around as a code word for the worst of it. Well, Mrs. Reeves lived at the far northwest side of Yamacraw. A huge oak tree and lovely cast iron and wooden bench were next to her apartment, and the Talmadge Bridge made a beautiful arch. She invited me in, then asked, "Want some cake?" I said, "Thank you, but…"

She asked again, "Want some cake?" I protested, "Oh, no, ma'am."

She asked again, more definitely, "You want some cake?" I finally surrendered and said, "Well, yes, thank you, Mrs. Reeves."

I would soon learn that this form of communication — Mrs. Addie Reeves telling you what you wanted even if you didn't know it at the time — was her standard operating procedure with a wide array of people.

Mrs. Reeves told me about herself: about coming to Savannah from Burke County — "the mule knew when to stop plowing at night;" about working for Savannah Sugar sewing sugar bags for 5 cents an hour; about working for Blanton's Travel Motel on Highway 17 — "they were good to me, but the day she said she couldn't pay me was the day I left;" and about walking to work and back everyday from Yamacraw to Port Wentworth, about seven miles.

Mrs. Reeves told me about being the oldest member of Connor's Temple. About the pastor's wife's hemline "too high!" and about meeting Waddie Welcome's father Henry in the 1920s. "He was a deacon and told me to stop betting. I told him I wasn't gambling, I was just playing bolita, and he told me that was too gambling."

Mrs. Reeves told me that Waddie's mother, Carrie, who died in 1974, had asked her to watch over her son. Mrs. Reeves was now 85 and clearly loved Mr. Welcome. But she was a better worrier and lover than she was a bureaucracy chaser.

For the next few months, I continued looking for a citizen advocate for Mr. Welcome — someone who would try to get him "back here" and then "back home."

In September of 1987, I called Lester Johnson, who I had met through Leadership Savannah in the early 1980s. After he'd heard Mr. Welcome's story, he said he would meet him. He was, in fact, going to be in Brunswick, halfway between Savannah and Abbeyville, the next week. We agreed to meet in Brunswick and drive to Abbeyville together to meet Mr. Welcome.

Lester Johnson, in his Broughton Street law office in Savannah, Georgia. A native of Savannah, Mr. Johnson maintains a large private practice and is also retained as Assistant City Attorney for the City of Savannah. He is a recent past president of the Savannah Bar Association.

Driving back home there was no question. Lester would get Mr. Welcome back to Savannah. That would turn out to mean meeting Mrs. Reeves, making a lot of phone calls, filling out paperwork for a local nursing home in Port Wentworth — and, at the last minute, paying $300 for the ambulance ride back to Savannah from Abbeyville. This all happened in a couple of months' time.

Bringing Mr. Welcome back to Savannah set the stage for a much longer journey, bringing him back home.

From the mid 1980s through the early '90s, Mr. Welcome lived in nursing homes. Lester, as his citizen advocate, became his representative payee to guide his financial affairs; acquired medical power of attorney after an incident when an E.R. doctor at a local hospital tried to put a "Do Not Resuscitate" order on Mr. Welcome. A staff person at the hospital called Lester, who with his friend, Jeff Alden, spent several hours on a Saturday laying out medical options to Mr. Welcome, making sure he understood. They asked questions with yes or no answers so that they were sure they understood what Mr. Welcome wanted in terms of advance directives. Lester also had an abusive staff member reassigned at a nursing home. He continued to listen to Mr. Welcome very carefully — by checking and double-checking his understanding of Mr. Welcome's answers, which were a mixture of sound and motion.

So Mr. Welcome was living in Savannah in a nursing home, and an increasing number of people were getting to know him and one another through being involved in citizen advocacy. Then Mr. Welcome connected with a small group of people who called themselves The Storytellers.

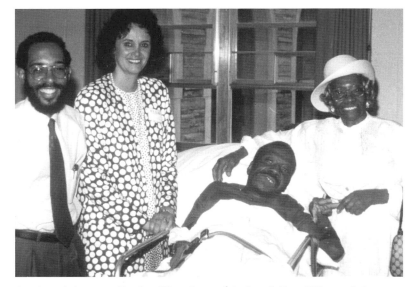

Lester Johnson, Becky Cheatham (chair of the Citizen Advocacy board and Chief Superior Court Judge Frank Cheatham's wife), Mr. Welcome and Mrs. Reeves at one of our annual meetings.

This picture catches Mrs. Reeves in the act of using one of her most powerful tools of hospitality: pitching peppermints at people. Mrs. Reeves always traveled with peppermints, dozens and dozens of peppermints, to give or toss to friends, acquaintances and soon-to-be acquaintances.

Mr. Welcome with his brother, Willie. Willie was the only other Welcome brother who stayed in Savannah. The other three left for larger cities with less segregation and more opportunity – a very common story among young black men and women of their generation. Right after this photo was taken, Mr. Willie Welcome passed on. Because Willie could understand some of what Waddie said, this was a great loss. As you see here, Mr. Welcome is beginning to look more like a jazz musician with his signature shades.

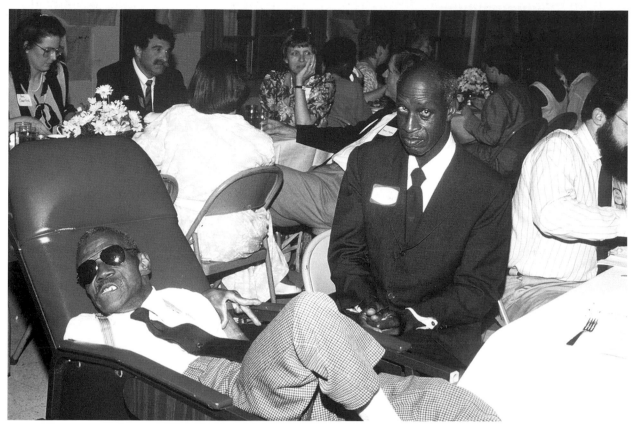

Jane Fishman, a local column writer for the *Savannah Morning News,* got to know and admire Mrs. Reeves' cooking and character. Jane tended a big garden near Mrs. Reeves' house and would take collard greens and other good things by. She got to know Mr. Welcome as well, and introduced them both to Ms. Carmela Aliffi, an art teacher at St. Vincent's Academy and to Gene Downs, arts editor for the *Savannah Morning News.* Ms. Albertha Parker who Mr. Welcome was living with is to his immediate right. Gradually, Mr. Welcome was meeting more people and becoming better known.

The Storytellers

— Susan Earl

Mrs. Mizelle Harrison, Alethia Reddick, Jeanette Mereski and Jackie Immel at a Saturday work session for The Storytellers at the Bull Street Baptist Church.

SUSAN EARL

In 1993, I became one of the founding members of a grass roots organization called The Storytellers. It was loosely modeled on the style of meetings at the Highlander Folk School* in Tennessee, where people sat in a circle in rocking chairs.

In our monthly meetings in the social hall of the St. James Catholic Church, we listened to each other's stories and learned each other's dreams. The church provided hospitality with an attractive and comfortable place to eat a covered-dish meal each time we met. Georgia Infirmary provided lift-equipped transportation to help some people attend. The power of eating together was acknowledged by members as an important basis of our group's solidarity. People helped each other — cooking, serving and eating. After dinner, everyone moved from tables to the large open area where we formed a circle. Members took turns leading the meeting, and each time we met one of us got to tell the long story of our life. It wasn't easy to reveal our fears, hopes and dreams, but respectful listening was deliberately practiced. Someone always took notes on chart paper. Little by little, we got to know each other. The Storytellers helped to form support systems that assisted many of our members who were living in nursing homes to move toward community life. In addition, the associational lives of all of the members gradually changed through participation in this process.

Gillian Grable was known around the state for her work in person-centered planning. We asked her to come to Savannah for a series of Saturday work sessions. We invited members of The Storytellers who were anxious to work on developing circles of support as a first step in planning for lives outside of nursing homes. Waddie Welcome was one of the people in that first work session. I agreed to be in his group. At that point we didn't know much about Mr. Welcome except what we had learned from Mrs. Reeves and Lester Johnson. We knew Mr. Welcome couldn't read, and we thought he couldn't speak. We didn't know if he had any family still living. What we did know was that Mr. Welcome was miserable living in the nursing home; he was able to make it clear that he wanted OUT.

* Highlander is legendary as the place where much of the strategy of the civil rights movement was forged. "We Shall Overcome," the anthem of the movement, was first sung there. Myles Horton, one of the original founders of Highlander in the 1930s, understood the importance of creating a space for people to learn and gain personal strength by hearing about each other's experiences.

At a work session at the Bull Street Baptist Church, Jeff Alden records an idea from The Storytellers group as young Alice Kohler critiques.

In the corner of the Bull Street Baptist Church social hall that Saturday morning, Waddie Welcome, Debra Selman, Tom Lamar, Jeff Alden, Dotti Black and I tried to learn more about what Mr. Welcome wanted. He challenged us to develop a method to understand him. As a group we quickly learned he could reliably answer "yes" or "no" questions. By giving him yes and no options to choose from, he could paint a clear picture of what he wanted his life to be like. We took turns writing and drawing on large sheets of newsprint attached to the walls with masking tape. Mr. Welcome was delighted to see his life and ideas validated in those drawings. They were like a series of light bulbs — new ideas, new possibilities — illuminated for all of us. Later we used the wall-paper to help us remember and explain what we had discovered.

We tried to see the real Waddie Welcome and value him. We worked to define and understand the roles he could play if given the opportunity: historian — he had seen a lot of history in his 79 years; teacher — if we could figure out how to understand what he had to tell us; dreamer — if he could still hold on to his dreams, we'd like to learn how he had done it; and community-builder — we had no idea how very prophetic that idea would be.

When we got it right, he would reward us with a laugh and a delighted grin so big it spurred us on to discover more. Like assembling a puzzle, the more pieces we put together, the more we wanted to do.

Sometimes when we got it wrong, he laughed. He rarely got frustrated. And the group process worked — when one of us bogged down, another would have an idea. We left that day with several prizes: knowing we had cracked the communication challenge, learning that he was a determined man who wanted to live in a house with a family with children where he could smell good home-cooking. We knew the biggest prize was that if we as a group could figure out how to make it work for Waddie Welcome — a 79-year-old man with cerebral palsy who couldn't move or speak and who had outlived his parents and siblings — then there wasn't anyone in the state of Georgia who was too old or too disabled to live in the community.

We left with assignments. Some of us would talk with Mrs. Reeves and to Deacon Washington Hart from Mr. Welcome's church, Connors Temple. One of us would research the Medicaid waiver programs and what services they could offer.

Mr. Welcome with Debra Selman, facilitator of Mr. Welcome's circle.

We 'went walking' with Mr. W. W. Law who was born in the Cuyler-Brownville community in 1923. As a child, Mr. Law saw his mother treated disrespectfully at the hand of a public official. This led to a lifetime of civil rights and civic activism starting with membership, then leadership, in the NAACP Youth Council in high school and college. In 1949, after a three year stint in the Army, Mr. Law returned to Savannah to work as a letter carrier in Cuyler-Brownville. In September of 1961, he was chased from this job by Congressman G. Elliot Hagan, only to be quickly reinstated by President John F. Kennedy.

Mr. Law never owned a car and walked everywhere, even though he was now in his 70s. He knew the Cuyler community like the back of his hand and remembered the Welcome family from his letter-carrying days. We asked if he would help us find out if there were people still left who would have known Henry and Carrie Welcome and their children. Walking from house to house, he would call out a name then step up onto the porch. A voice from inside the house would call back, and a moment later we would be in the living room. There would be a short personal conversation between Mr. Law and our impromptu hostess and then on to asking about the Welcome family: "Do you remember them? What house did they live in? Who else were they related to? What were their childrens' names? Where did they go to school? Who lived next door? Across the street? Who knew them the best? Who else would know?"

Mr. W. W. Law in Savannah, Georgia.

REGION 18

Chatham/Effingham Regional Board
for Mental Health/Mental Retardation/Substance Abuse

Telephone: (912) 652-3530
Gist: 361-3530 Gist Fax: 361-3538
Fax: (912) 652-3538

Midtown Medical Center, Suite 1
Drayton & 33rd Streets
Savannah, Georgia 31401

Catherine E. McRae
Executive Director

BOARD
MEMBERS:
James F. Bass, Jr.
Russell L. Billings
Thea Edwards
Gussie A. Nease
David L. Saussy
Annie H. Welch

May 9, 1996

Mrs. Susan Earl
Georgia Infirmary Day Center
  for Rehabilitation
1900 Abercorn Street
Savannah, GA 31401

Dear Susan:

I have read your brochure regarding the Circle of Friends appreciation for Chatham Nursing Home resident, Waddy Welcome. I understand that he has been referred to the Comprehensive Evaluation Team for evaluation for the Mental Retardation Waiver Program.

Our Regional Board is also an advocate for all consumers with disabilities of mental illness, mental retardation and substance abuse. We rely on the recommendations of the CET for the priorities for the MRWP Program. We have recently been notified that all MRWP slots have been frozen at the '96 level.

Sincerely,

xc: Rep. Regina Thomas
    Sharon Mills, CET
    Tom Hodgson

Debra Selman
1900 Lincoln Street
Savannah, GA 31401

May 23, 1996

Chairman

Savannah, GA 31410

Dear

Thank you for your letter of May 9. Let me reframe our position regarding Mr. Welcome.

1. We have case management and allied services identified.

2. We have an ever growing group of citizens willing to act in whatever way necessary as citizens.

3. What Mr. Welcome needs is funding,--- not evaluations, not a place on a waiting list, and not another lukewarm letter with all sorts of factual errors from you.

May I suggest that a meeting be set up between board members, Judge James Bass, David Saussy, and Annie Welch (2 of the 3 would be fine) and people from Mr. Welcome's circle. Thus, surely a face to face meeting focusing on dramatic, positive action can move this along.

Timing is critical. Mr. Welcome continues to be in danger in the nursing home. We would like to meet prior to June 6th. You can reach me at

Sincerely,

Debra Selman

Debra Selman

cc: Regional Board Members
    Catherine McRae
    Sharon Mills
    Mr. Welcome's Circle Members

Debra Selman - Group Facilitator	Archie Gadson	Rep. Regina Thomas
Susan Earl	Mary Deloach	Jeff and Cathy Alden
Deacon Hart	Naomi Brown	Henry and Donna Moore
Addie Reeves	Dorothy and George Futch	Rev. B. R. Mitchell, Jr.
Lester Johnson	Tom Lamar	W. W. Law
Brenda Bell	Jackie Immel	Deacon Miller
Dan Weatherly	Dotti and Paul Black	
Jan Williamson	Clarence Peterson	
Robert Butts	Sylvia Kemp	

Speaking through the screen of a street-level window of a modest rowhouse, Mr. Law briefly visited and then asked these same questions of a woman as she lay in bed. As we walked away I asked, "Who takes care of her?" He stopped, and with outstretched arm, waved out across the narrow unpaved street and said, "These people, these people take care of her." Without a word, we walked on to the next front porch.

Debra Selman, galvanized into becoming a disability rights activist by a near miss on nursing home placement herself, became the circle facilitator. She researched Mr. Welcome's family in copies of Savannah's "Colored City Directory" in the public library dating back to 1910. She helped him send Christmas cards to old and new acquaintances to strengthen and enlarge the circle. She badgered Congressman Jack Kingston until he sent a representative to visit Mr. Welcome in the nursing home, and she reminded other circle members of their "to dos." She was the one who kept the momentum going. Circle members didn't want to have to admit to Debra that they had failed to complete their assignments.

Along the way we added members to the circle: State Representative Regina Thomas; Sylvia Kemp, who would provide a place for Mr. Welcome in her home; Herman and Linda Friedman, local business people; Deacon Hart; and Jane Fishman, columnist for the *Savannah Morning News*. Several of Mr. Welcome's great-nieces — Margaret Welcome Jackson and Mary Welcome Williams and her sons, Mario and Andre joined the circle.

On one Christmas Day, Lester Johnson, a Muslim, and my daughter and I, who are Jewish, visited Mr. Welcome in the nursing home and laughed at the strength our circle's multi-culturalism had given us. Mr. Welcome beamed from his preferred place in the hallway near the nurses' station. An astute observer of human nature and a connoisseur of the female form, he commented on the flow of people and events with an arch of one eyebrow, a quick thrust of his tongue; he had a lexicon of language in his face.

We watched Mr. Welcome use his body to draw a line in the sand. How someone treated him physically was an important factor in the way he determined which side of the line they were on. Glib words and pats on the head didn't cut it. Helping him shift positions in the uncomfortable "geriatric" chair — provided by the nursing home in lieu of a wheelchair — was a better test of

Mr. Welcome looking forward with excitement
to life outside the nursing home.

friendship than posturing. The pretenders got "the look" — rolled eyes followed them as they continued down the hall. He shot us one of his smiles, and gave us that great laugh.

It took the circle almost two years to figure out how to get Mr. Welcome out of the nursing home, including winning the fight for him to be considered eligible for the Medicaid waiver program. It took polite threats and subtle coercion, but it got done. It didn't hurt that Mr. Welcome's circle now included among its members a state representative, the president of the Savannah Bar Association, a revered civil rights leader and historian, and a newspaper reporter.

The Medicaid waiver paid a provider agency for Mr. Welcome's personal care services. The circle was fortunate to work with an agency that could see itself in partnership with Mr. Welcome and his supporters. Their receptivity to new ways of doing things opened the way to success. With funding for in-home services secured, Mr. Welcome moved in with friends, Jeff and Kathy Alden until his dream of a family home with children could be found.

I was there when Jeff wheeled Mr. Welcome out the front door of the nursing home and sat him in the front seat of his truck. My 10-year-old daughter and her friend helped make up Mr. Welcome's bed at Jeff and Kathy's. I took the pictures, and I'll always treasure that afternoon. After all the talking, it was simple, it was quiet, but it was radical social change.

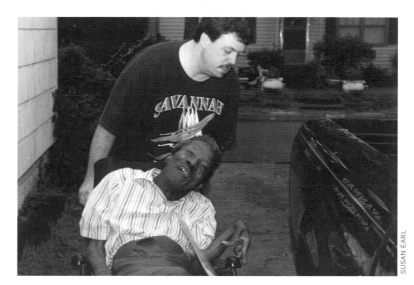

Jeff and Mr. Welcome coming home to Jeff and Kathy's house.

Keeping the Social
in Social Change

— Tom Kohler

SUSAN EARL

Small elevator, strong men: Kim Abbot helps
Mr. Welcome up four flights of stairs.

"We started off meeting and talking together, then we progressed to having parties." This comes from Susan Earl, who as a teenager was running the mimeo machine for the Student Peace Union in the room next to Bayard Rustin and A.J. Muste at the Fellowship of Reconciliation in New York City as they planned the pivotal 1963 Civil Rights March on Washington. This is where Martin Luther King Jr.'s "I Have a Dream" speech called the country to conscience. Susan is not a novice, a newcomer to social change. At the University of Wisconsin during the 1960s she was active with the Committee to End the War in Vietnam.

"We progressed to having parties" mirrors the wisdom of two Savannah citizens. Neel Foster, citizen advocate, homemaker, parent and visual artist, says, "You have to keep the 'social' in social change." W.W. Law echoed that sentiment when I asked him "What scares you the most these days?" He answered, "People are so busy going to meetings they don't have time to visit."

In 1996, the University of Georgia asked to make a documentary film about Mr. Welcome, his allies and supporters. Mr. Welcome agreed. Narcel Reedus shot and Gillian Grable produced the video, "Waddie Welcome: A Man Who Cannot Be Denied." It won film festival awards around the country.

The video previewed at the Jimmy Carter Center in Atlanta to a crowd of about 300 people including a great turnout from legislators. And then it premiered at the Ralph Mark Gilbert Civil Rights Museum in Savannah. The museum screening room holds 75 people, and we expected that number. But instead 150 people turned out. So the crowd had to split into two showings, and people had to get up and down the four flights of stairs or take the too-small elevator.

Mr. Welcome and his friends and allies won the TASH (The Association of People with Severe Handicaps) Collaboration Award in 1998, and Mr. Welcome went to Seattle, Washington, to receive it.

Mr. Welcome and a couple of his friends worked together to tape his acceptance speech:

> My name is Waddie Welcome, and I thank you for this honor. I have been blessed to have family, neighbors, church and friends. My oldest friend, my deepest friend, is Mrs. Addie Reeves. She is 97 years old and told me that if God had meant for her to fly, she would have had wings... so she didn't come to be with you today.
>
> I hope that you can learn some of life's lessons from the video, "Waddie Welcome: A Man Who Cannot Be Denied." In the video you will see Mrs. Reeves and a woman named Debra Selman. Don't try to cross them! That's a lesson that a lot of people in Savannah have learned.
>
> Again, thank you for this honor.

A Christmas party at Dotti Black's house. From left: Debra Selman, Mr. Welcome, young Emily Earl and Deacon Morris.

The Carter Center preview of *Waddie Welcome: A Man Who Cannot Be Denied.* From left: Susan Earl, Tom Kohler, Sylvia Kemp, Dotti Black, Debra Selman and young friends.

Mary Welcome Williams, one of Mr. Welcome's great nieces, at the premiere.

At the Carter Center preview in Atlanta, Mr. Welcome was,
as usual, attracting the women.

Mr. Welcome and Tom Kohler
on the plane to Seattle.

Waddie Welcome and Gillian Grable
at the TASH Conference.

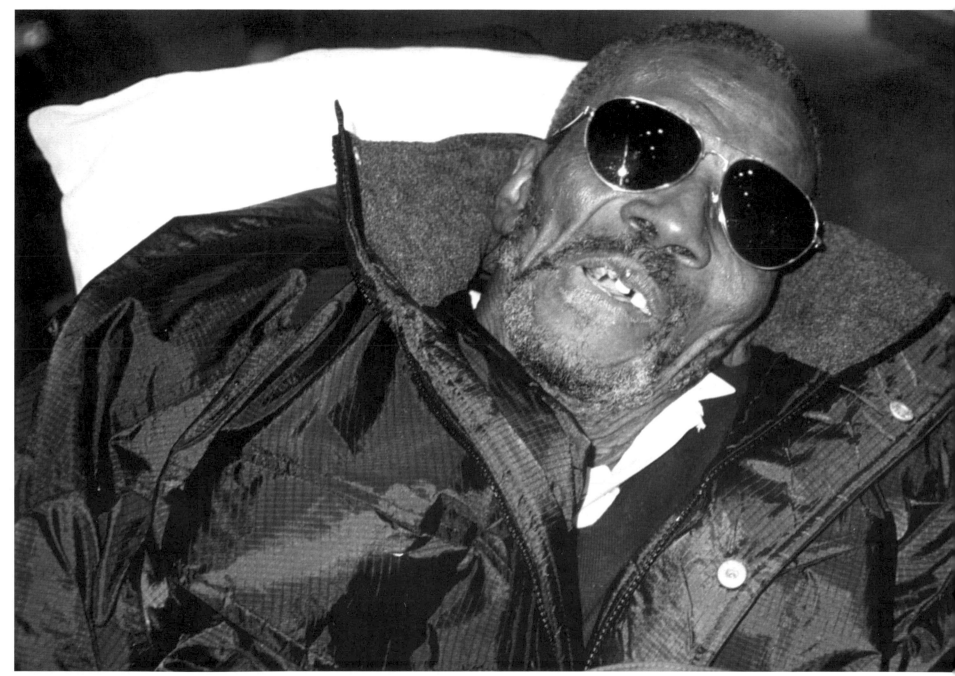

Mr. Welcome sightseeing in Seattle.

Gillian Grable married Judge Johnny Mason, and Mr. Welcome traveled to Atlanta to attend the wedding and reception.

Mr. Welcome with Gillian's husband, Judge Johnny Mason. Mr. Welcome came to know an increasing number of influential political and legal figures around the state.

Mr. Welcome and friends hosted a birthday party for Mrs. Reeves 96th birthday at the home of Jane Fishman. Yes, Mrs. Reeves did manage to blow out all 96 candles.

Mr. Welcome and Jeff Alden brave the rain together.

Mrs. Reeves, women from her Mission Circle at Connor's Temple, State Representative Regina Thomas and Deacon Hart.

Born on the Fourth of July in 1914

Mr. Walt (Waddie) Welcome will celebrate his 85th Birthday this Sunday. Waddie, family and friends invite you to...

- Join him at church at 11:00 am Sunday morning at Conners Temple Baptist Church on the corner of Martin Luther King, Jr. and West Gwinnett Streets.

  Come to the home of Mrs. Addie Reeves at 617 West Gwinnett on Sunday afternoon between 4:00 p.m. and 6:00 p.m. for good food, singing and an amazing birthday cake... *moved to Jane Fishman's Garden.*

Your being there makes it a party!!!!

The Welcome family gave Mr. Welcome a handmade afghan and a big cake. Several generations of extended family came to celebrate.

Then on July 4th, a big 85th birthday party was given for Mr. Welcome.

Hostess Ms. Jane Fishman and the man of honor share a laugh.

Happy Birthday!

Connect Savannah

— Tom **Kohler**

SHAWN BALDWIN

John Berendt

▶ He wrote "The Book." Need we say more?

The stories of this city's eccentrics included in "Midnight in the Garden of Good and Evil" were not fresh to perennial Savannahians.

They had heard them hashed and rehashed at cocktail parties and in barbershops for years.

But when author John Berendt shared Savannah's whimsical characters with the world, something big happened. The world became hopelessly intrigued and wanted even more.

By the thousands, people came. They came to gaze upon Mercer House and to listen to Emma Kelly sing at Hannah's. They came to see the Lady Chablis perform at Club One, and they came to stroll the grounds of Bonaventure Cemetery and have a martini on Conrad Aiken's grave.

Cash accompanied their curiosity, and Savannah benefited as much from the sale of "The Book" as did its writer and publisher.

Berendt has sold more than three million hardbacks and paperbacks since the novel was published in 1994. While it is impossible to attach such a specific number to Savannah's intake, even the book's detractors acknowledge it has enriched the city.

You cannot say that Berendt put Savannah on the map; this wonderful city was already a destination for tourists who loved old and beautiful things.

What the book did, though, was open up Savannah to everyone else. These post-book years have been a boon for touring companies, inns, gift shops and eateries. Millions have been made by these proprietors, but the prosperity transcends money.

For all of her exposure, Savannah has been able to maintain her moss-covered mystery. The tourists come, they see, but they cannot package the city's subtlety and romance for their suitcases.

How unusual it is that a city can receive so much without having to lose anything.

John Duncan, a historian/shopkeeper who was first befriended by Berendt during the author's eight years of research and writing, said the writer has not only made the biggest difference in Savannah during the past decade, but perhaps in the past century.

He said the book is the impression the world will have of Savannah for perhaps forever.

"I have only heard two negative comments about the book: one person said it was vulgar, and the other person said it was trash," Duncan said. "That's two bad comments out of three million books sold. Not bad.

"John Berendt certainly did not set out to cast any bad light on Savannah. He came to town with his tape recorder and let the people hang themselves if they so chose."

The book did depict acts of passions run amuck, outlandish personalities and criminal behavior accepted by the general public because of the culprit's place in society. Some Savannahians did take exception to that.

In some circles, one is considered either as pro-book or anti-book.

Attorney Sonny Seiler, who defended antiques dealer Jim Williams (the central character of the book) on charges of murdering Danny Hansford, said initially Berendt did not set out to do a story on Savannah. He wanted to write a book on Williams' trials, but he had limited access to the jailed defendant.

That is when Berendt decided to unite all of the controversial tales he was hearing with court happenings.

"There are two classes of people in Savannah who look at that book, and what it all boils down to is whose ox is in the ditch," Seiler said. "If the book stepped on your toes or someone you respect, you think it is an abhorrence. If it did not and you are entertained by it, then you think it is a great book.

"The only doubt I ever had about it was if it would be accepted outside of Savannah. If you wrote a book on Trenton, N.J., I wouldn't buy the damn book because I am not interested in what fascinating stories you can tell me of Trenton, N.J."

— *Patricia C. Stumb*

Connect Savannah, December 4, 1999.

In December 1999, the newspaper, *Connect Savannah,* ran an issue about the 10 most influential people of the decade in Savannah. John Berendt got in because he wrote 'the book,' "Midnight in the Garden of Good and Evil."

U.S. Representative Jack Kingston was one of the 10 most influential. The citation reads: "His integrity generates broad political support." And Mr. Waddie Welcome was one of the 10 as well.

Waddie Welcome, a surprising new leader. At first glance Waddie Welcome looks anything but influential, beset with cerebral palsy and approaching nine full decades, he is mostly quiet and unassuming. But beneath the years, beneath the persona of disability, lies fierce determination, a determination that has influenced thousands across the state, the nation and the world.

After ten years of labor and toil, Mr. Welcome and his friends and allies won. He left nursing home life and moved in with a host family in Savannah, Georgia. Word traveled of this charismatic and determined man and the University of Georgia Center for Human Development produced a video about Mr. Welcome's story, his better

living conditions and most importantly, how he influenced those around him.

Mr. Welcome's message was ripe for Medicaid laws that had grown ineffective and obsolete. In hopes of lobbying legislators, copies were forwarded to state representatives.

Hunter Hurst, Chairman of the Governor's Blue Ribbon Task Force on Community Services, said, "Mr. Welcome's video was used repeatedly to help create a political environment much more friendly to community services and other options to nursing homes."

Ironically, Mr. Welcome has used the very thing that has handicapped him since birth – his body. He uses it to raise awareness and mobilize action.

By pushing his own agenda, he is now pushing public policy. By pushing public policy, he is making an impact for future generations. His message has a growing audience, not only in his city and state, but nationally and internationally.

Waddie Welcome, a man of few words, an agent of change, a surprising new leader.

— Timothy Daiss, *Connect Savannah*

MATT MOYER

Jack Kingston

▶ His integrity generates broad political support

Facing a traditionally hostile audience, Jack Kingston, a slim statesman with a boy-next-door face, works his usual magic. Words fall from his mouth, arranging themselves without any rush whatsoever, into amusing stories.

The measured, down-home style seems suited to a farmer chatting at a local diner before gulping down a bitter cup of Joe and heading out to his fields. Certainly, the message hasn't come from a power-wielding Washington politician.

But Kingston is no ordinary U.S. Congressman. "Even if you don't like him, you trust him," says longtime friend and political ally State Sen. Eric Johnson. "Even if you don't like his ideology, you respect him."

As Kingston looks out on a sea of African-American, staunchly Democratic faces, he starts talking about school prayer. Heads begin nodding in agreement.

"Even the black population, which usually has nothing to do with Republicans, likes him," Johnson says. "It's his sincerity; that's what they respect. You see so little of it in politicians these days."

Some call it Kingston's "aw shucks" persona. Others refer more directly to the attributes that won him an "unwinnable" Congressional seat and have kept him in office for seven years. They use words like dedication, sincerity and commitment

"It's obvious from being with and knowing Jack, he represents what all of us are looking for in this day and time: a man with good, solid family values," says Tom Coleman, who was recently named Commissioner for the Georgia Department of Transportation. A Savannah businessman and experienced politician, Coleman has held various state and local offices. Both men, for example, served in the Georgia General Assembly. Kingston became a state representative at 29. And in 1992 he took over stewardship of the First Congressional District. He captured a seat that had belonged, for as long as anyone cared to remember, to a Democrat. "Jack gave up a House seat to run for a Congressional seat that no one thought a Republican could ever win," says Johnson, who managed Kingston's congressional campaign

Repeatedly endorsed by his constituents, Kingston now sits on the powerful Appropriations Committee in the U.S. House of Representatives. He's won relief for local farmers, lucrative federal contracts for Savannah and Brunswick manufacturers, increased public access to Plum Orchard on Cumberland Island, approval for improvements to barracks at Fort Stewart, funding for construction of a vital bridge in Brunswick and the go-ahead for harbor dredging in Savannah. Supporters, however, say his influence transcends local efforts. Federal belt-tightening, balancing the budget and limiting big government are all part of Kingston's

legacy.

"Jack is a very able statesman," says Coleman. "He's outgoing. He's certainly a person who follows up on things. I think people appreciate the personal attention they feel they can get from him." This year, Kingston assisted 4,000 residents from his district.

Maintaining a schedule that would leave most people exhausted, he commutes almost every weekend to Savannah. His wife Libby, who friends describe as a partner in Jack's political career, was a former student government president at the University of Georgia—Athens. The couple met while working on a presidential campaign and have remained plugged into politics ever since. The Kingstons have four children. Jack, now 44, says the time he spends helping his kids with their homework is as important as his hours within the Beltway.

Kingston's mother helped spawn his early interest in politics. By sixth or seventh grade, Jack already knew it was the career path for him. A family tragedy, the death of his teen-age sister, also influenced the future Congressman. In the midst of the gut-wrenching pain, he acquired an empathy that still probably more than anything else comes across to the people he represents.

"It's a defining moment in your life," Kingston says about his sister's untimely death. "It probably made me a lot more sensitive. It makes you far more sympathetic to anybody who has a problem."

In his characteristically self-effacing manner, Kingston says he's isn't sure why those from both sides of the political aisle like him. "I know one thing people have said, they're glad I haven't turned Washington," he says. "I see myself as a normal American."

While his unpretentious demeanor assists in building local support, Kingston's still a savvy politician who knows how to get results.

"Playing on the team that I think has brought some real changes in Washington has been a great honor," he says. A rising star, he's now wrestling with the choice between climbing through the ranks in the House or pursuing a longtime dream of running for the Senate.

Coleman, for one, thinks Kingston will succeed with whatever he chooses. And Johnson agrees.

"It's a combination of his integrity, it's a Reagan-esque belief in his ideology," Johnson says about Kingston's broad-based, non-partisan popularity. "He doesn't have to take a poll or conduct a survey, it just comes from his gut."

Grassroots backing helped carry Kingston onto the national stage. Where he'll ultimately end up appears — if his supporters are correct — very promising indeed. Be assured, however, that he'll still pull on weathered boots and tromp through onion fields alongside concerned farmers. Summing up the Kingston mystique, Johnson adds, "He has a real ability to connect with people."

Ann Ladd

Connect Savannah, December 4, 1999.

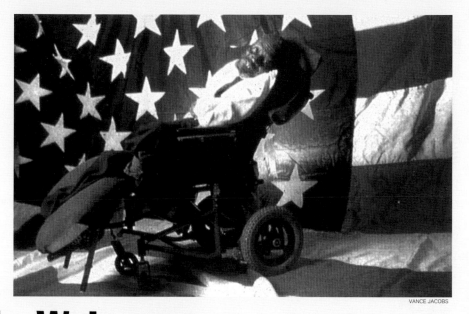

VANCE JACOBS

Waddie Welcome ▸ A surprising new leader

At first glance Waddie Welcome looks anything but influential, beset with cerebral palsy, and approaching nine full decades, he is mostly quiet and unassuming. But beneath the years, beneath the persona of disability, lies fierce determination, a determination that has influenced thousands across the state, the nation, and the world.

In spite of having lived through the Civil Rights movement of the 1960s and the disability rights movement of the 1980s, Welcome found himself living in a nursing home with horrific conditions.

Yet, Welcome has been blessed with what is called a circle of friends, people, often advocates, coming together with the goal of helping one particular individual. Members listen, tell their stories, share their hopes, their dreams. Some call this person-centered planning, but it's just community, people helping people.

For the most part, Welcome speaks little, but his friends learned how to communicate with him, learned his language. By doing so, they discovered his determination to move back into the community. And, finally, after 10 years of labor and toil, the mission was successful; Mr. Welcome moved into a private home with a host family.

It is said that luck is when opportunity meets preparation. If so, then Mr. Welcome has forged his own luck. In 1996 The Center for Human Development at the University of Georgia wanted to produce a video on disabilities and aging. Soon, word spread about a determined black man with cerebral palsy who had met and challenged many odds. Intrigued, they produced a documentary about Mr. Welcome's story, his better living conditions, and most important, how he

influenced those around him.

The documentary premiered to a packed house at the Carter Center in Atlanta on the night of July 19, 1997. Locally, it premiered at the Ralph Mark Gilbert Civil Rights Museum. With only 100 seats to fill, 300-plus arrived, resulting in two standing room only viewings. By night's end, both audiences were encouraged and enthusiastic. It appeared that this unlikely man, often overlooked in the affairs of men, was on his way to notoriety.

Mr. Welcome's message was ripe for Medicaid laws that had grown ineffective and obsolete. In hopes of lobbying legislators, copies were forwarded to state representatives. Said Hunter Hurst, chairman of the Governor's Blue Ribbon Task Force on Community Services. "Mr. Welcome's video was used repeatedly to help create a political environment much more friendly to

community services and options to nursing homes."

But the momentum would not stop. Last year Welcome's video won the 1998 Collaboration Award from TASH, the premiere advocacy organization for people with severe handicaps. Since then, Welcome's video has won three additional awards.

Ironically, Mr. Welcome has used the very thing that has handicapped him since birth, his body. He used it to raise awareness and mobilize action. By pushing his own agenda, he is now pushing public policy. By pushing public policy, he is making an impact for future generations. His message now has a growing audience, not only in his city and state, but nationally, and internationally.

Waddie Welcome, a man of few words, an agent of change, a surprising new leader.

– Timothy Daiss

Connect Savannah, December 4, 1999.

"Go on soldier,
take your rest."

— Susan Earl

In November 2000, after living in four different family homes, Mr. Welcome decided he wanted to move back in with Jeff Alden. They had continued to be close over the years. As a nurse and a long-time friend, Jeff was familiar with the care that Mr. Welcome needed. Among the things they had in common were their faith, sense of humor, appreciation of attractive women and a love of "shoot-em-up" Westerns. He converted the sunny front room of his Eastside Savannah house into a bedroom where Mr. Welcome could look out at the oak trees in the yard. He built a ramp and found a used GMC Safari van with a wheelchair lift. They were looking forward to having some good times.

Mr. Welcome had been having some health problems, which resulted in hospitalization. The circle members were surprised when his health suddenly deteriorated and he was placed in the intensive care unit on a ventilator.

All of December, he remained in the ICU. We took turns visiting every day, six visits a day, for 29 days. It was intense. Jeff brought Mrs. Reeves; the nieces and their children came. Alberta Parker, with whom Mr. Welcome had lived with before moving to

Jeff's, came almost every day. Lester Johnson chose Mr. Welcome's cardiologist and asked him to oversee his hospital care because they both attended the same small mosque. We all agreed this was a key decision in ensuring the best care for Mr. Welcome.

Debra brought a bulletin board for Mr. Welcome's ICU room to display photos of him with Congressman Jack Kingston and other prominent civic leaders. A scrapbook of newspaper articles, pictures and stories about Mr. Welcome was placed on the workspace just outside his room where doctors and nurses stood to have informal consults. Nurses who gave good care were sent personal thank you notes, and letters were written to their supervisors. Word traveled quickly about hospital staff who seemed less skilled or unconcerned.

Lester, Debra, Jeff and I sat in a circle in the family waiting room and held hands. We prayed. We cried and hugged each other. We bargained. We did what all the other families were doing. We met with the doctors and were told that Mr. Welcome had liver cancer, and there was little chance of him going home from the hospital. We agreed that we'd be happy if Mr. Welcome could have just one day at home, off the ventilator. We thought we knew Mr. Welcome well enough to guess that would be what he wanted. We hoped we'd get the chance to ask him. And amazingly, we did.

Beating the odds as he had done his entire life, Waddie Welcome improved enough to be taken off the ventilator. He could breathe on his own. A week later he was able to go home. We knew the cancer was fast-moving. The oncologist in meeting with the four of us had said, two, three months, maybe. Although we feared he would spend his last few days in awful pain, that did not happen.

When Jeff called me at 2:30 a.m. to tell me to come over right away, I was a little surprised. Earlier that night when I had visited, Mr. Welcome hadn't seemed so bad. But when I got there, his breathing was very rapid and shallow, and I agreed with Jeff that although I had never seen anyone dying, it did seem like that was what was happening. Mr. Welcome was going to teach us one last lesson.

Jeff and I sat on either side of his recliner and touched him gently, reassuring him we were there, although he didn't show any response. The red, white and blue birthday afghan covered his legs. Except for the sound of Jeff's deep voice reading psalms from the Bible, "He leadeth me beside the still waters, He restoreth my soul," it was very quiet.

Faye Jones, who had done Mr. Welcome's morning care every day, came in about an hour later. She clearly knew him well and loved him. Faye took my place rubbing Mr. Welcome's forehead. I sat and rubbed his feet. His breathing was shallow, but he seemed peaceful. We told him we loved him and we knew he had to go, and that it was okay. Faye said over and over, "Go on soldier, take your rest." What a perfect word for Mr. Welcome. He was a soldier in many ways.

In the early morning, Jeff and Faye gently carried Mr. Welcome from his Lazy Boy to his bed. Jeff hadn't slept since the night before, so we sent him to lie down. I sat in Mr. Welcome's recliner; Faye stood by him. In minutes, Faye said, "Susan, go get Jeff." We got back to Mr. Welcome and stood, all touching him. He breathed several times, then stopped. Jeff put his palm on his chest and said, "He's gone." I could not believe it. A second earlier he was breathing and alive.

Waddie Welcome was born on July 4, 1914; he died January 14, Martin Luther King Holiday Sunday, 2001.

Homegoing

— Tom Kohler

Mr. Welcome's funeral was a fitting tribute to the man he was. The church was full of family, friends, circle and church members and people from all over Savannah whom Mr. Welcome had touched. They were black and white, young and old. Some walked into the church, some wheeled in. There were out-of-town guests. Gillian Grable and I spoke, and so did his niece, Margaret Welcome Jackson. Narcel Reedus, the filmmaker, was there. The choir sang and his pastor, Reverend Dr. Bennie Mitchell Jr., eulogized him. Mrs. Reeves, now 99, sat right up front.

Mr. Welcome got one of the "big guy" obituaries. This happens only three or four times a year in the Savannah paper. It read:

Waddie Welcome, disabled rights activist, 1914-2001: He got his wish to live where he could "smell food on a stove and could hear children playing."

Man with cerebral palsy got wish to live in real home.
Waddie Welcome didn't like nursing homes.

Cold, sterile conditions, strangers as caretakers and distance from friends and family seemed to harm the Savannah man more than the cerebral palsy he had since birth.

After all, Welcome had spent his first 70 years or so cared for by his parents, Henry and Carrie, then his brother, Willie. No day-care programs. No respite care. No institutions.

WADDIE WELCOME
Disabled rights activist
1914-2001

Man with cerebral palsy got wish to live in real home

Waddie Welcome, 86, was one of the longest living Americans with cerebral palsy.

Special to the Savannah Morning News

By Anne Hart
Savannah Morning News

Waddie Welcome didn't like nursing homes.

Cold, sterile conditions, strangers as caretakers and distance from friends and family seemed to harm the Savannah man more than the cerebral palsy he had since birth.

After all, Welcome had spent his first 70 years or so cared for by his parents, Henry and Carrie, then his brother, Willie. No day-care programs. No respite care. No institutions.

to live in regular homes with regular folks.

"What he wanted was to live with a family where he could smell food on a stove and could hear children playing," said Tom Kohler, coordinator Chatham-Savannah Citizen Advocacy Inc. and a Welcome supporter.

Although unable to talk well, Welcome made his point to nursing home visitors that he didn't like it there.

"We learned to pick up certain gestures," said Savannah attorney Lester Johnson. "It was always, 'I want to get out.'"

ing, Welcome used a wheelchair to attend celebrations around town, including the 1997 premiere of an award-winning documentary, "Waddie Welcome: A Man Who Could Not Be Denied."

The "sensual, gritty optimist" knew how to motivate people of diverse colors and classes, Kohler said.

"The thing that people are surprised at, is the depth and breadth of the people who care about him," Kohler said.

What people find more shocking it that a charismatic senior citizen with disabilities opened the

the Circle of Friends.

He spent the past roughly 15 years influencing public policy to be more personal and less institutional.

Welcome and his supporters were the subject of a documentary film "Waddie Welcome: A Man Who Can Not Be Denied," produced by the University of Georgia. The film has won top honors at three video and film festivals nationwide. The International Association of People with Severe Handicaps honored Welcome and several friend with its 1998 Collaboration Award in Seattle.

Just family, residents in and near his Cuyler-Brownville neighborhood and members of his church, Connor's Temple Baptist, pitching in to help a man whose limbs and mouth didn't work like most.

But parents die and siblings sometimes can't provide living conditions approved by well-intentioned neighbors.

Officials were notified and placed Welcome in the first of a series of health care facilities, where he spent the next 10 years.

But Welcome longed to live in a home. His wish motivated a group of community members.

Thanks to their work over the years, government assistance that once funded Welcome's nursing home stay was used to pay for him to live in regular homes with regular folks.

"What he wanted was to live with a family where he could smell food on a stove and could hear children playing," said Tom Kohler, coordinator Chatham-Savannah Citizen Advocacy Inc. and a Welcome supporter.

Although unable to talk well, Welcome made his point to nursing home visitors that he didn't like it there.

"We learned to pick up certain gestures," said Savannah attorney Lester Johnson. "It was always, 'I want to get out.'"

"When we finally did it, it was a great feeling 'cause he was so happy."

Welcome got himself back home, with various families, close to his favorite fried chicken and sweets of his longtime friend, Addie Reeves, 99.

"I took care of him as my son," Reeves said. "He came to church every Sunday. He came in smiling."

With institutional life behind him, Welcome thrived in the four or five Savannah homes he lived in for the past decade or so.

He became perhaps the oldest person nationwide with cerebral palsy until he died Sunday of liver cancer. Welcome was 86 and still at home.

A lover of women and socializing, Welcome used a wheelchair to attend celebrations around town, including the 1997 premiere of an award-winning documentary, "Waddie Welcome: A Man Who Could Not Be Denied."

The "sensual, gritty optimist" knew how to motivate people of diverse colors and classes, Kohler said.

"The thing that people are surprised at, is the depth and breadth of the people who care about him," Kohler said.

What people find more shocking is that a charismatic senior citizen with disabilities opened the door for others to live in families, not institutions.

"Anyone in a nursing home who prefers to live with a family can now do that because of him," Johnson said.

NARCEL REEDUS

NARCEL REEDUS

NARCEL REEDUS

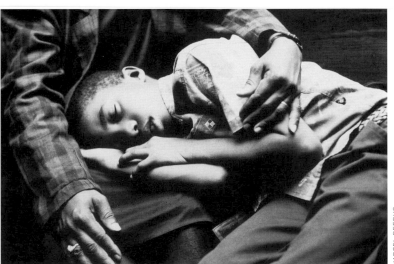

NARCEL REEDUS

Welcome found a way to live a real life. He found a way home.

Welcome, a native of Sylvania, lived much of his life in the Cuyler-Brownville neighborhood in Savannah. One of five boys, Welcome was never allowed to attend school because of his disability.

Welcome was named one of Chatham County's 10 most influential people of the decade in December 1999. He was a founding member of the St. James Storytellers Group and a member of the Circle of Friends.

He spent the past roughly 15 years influencing public policy to be more personal and less institutional.

Welcome and his supporters were the subject of a documentary film, "Waddie Welcome: A Man Who Can Not Be Denied," produced by the University of Georgia. The film has won top honors at three video and film festivals nationwide. The International Association of People with Severe Handicaps honored Welcome and several friends with its 1998 Collaboration Award in Seattle.

— Anne Hart, *Savannah Morning News*

After the funeral, we all went back to eat at the church and look at Mr. Welcome's pictures and tell Waddie Welcome stories. It may sound strange, but it was a wonderful day.

Lester Johnson told about how as a student at St. Mary's Catholic School in the 1950s, kids would go around the corner to a little corner store and get candy... and sometimes they would go to a house, where you could get things a little cheaper. But if you went there, you might see "the monster" — the monster being Waddie Welcome — watching over his mother's sale goods on the porch. He told old friends in town for a reunion about having re-met Mr. Welcome as an adult and about his stature in the community and beyond. They were, of course, more than a little surprised.

Mrs. Reeves took Mr. Welcome's passing hard, but her faith helped her. A broken hip at the age of 99 was too much. At the age of 100 years and 30 days, Mrs. Reeves passed on, over to a place she knew would be better.

After her death, the *Savannah Morning News* printed the following editorial:

They say that the good die young. They never met Mrs. Addie Reeves of Savannah. Mrs. Reeves, who died Monday this week at the age of 100, was living proof of the power of one. The longtime resident was well-known in her church, Connor's Temple, her neighborhood, mostly Yamacraw Village and Kayton Homes, and in the wider community for her generosity, strength, compassion and belief in human dignity.

NARCEL REEDUS

Mr. Welcome was carried to
Laurel Grove Cemetery where
his parents are buried.

Folks raised money to have a
marker erected at Mr. Welcome's
grave. Mary Welcome Williams and
her two boys — *Beloved son,
brother, uncle, friend and teacher.*

BILL DAWERS

NARCEL REEDUS

She touched and inspired hundreds, if not thousands, of people. She was best known for standing up for a former neighbor, Waddie Welcome, who was sent away to an out-of-town nursing home after his parents died. Mr. Welcome, who died a year ago at the age of 86, had cerebral palsy. He was a black man in a wheelchair who was easy to overlook. Mrs. Reeves had limited resources. But she also possessed a backbone of titanium. With the help of Chatham-Savannah Citizen Advocacy, she brought Mr. Welcome back to Savannah.

A native of Burke County, Mrs. Reeves was one of ten children who grew up on a farm and learned the value of work. And of cooking. If people went away hungry after sitting down at her table, it was their fault.

A funeral service is scheduled for 12:30 p.m. today at Connor's Temple with burial near the family homeplace. While her death is sad, her life is a cause for celebration. If this one woman changed her corner of the world, think of what could happen if others followed her example.

Here were her lessons of life: Live and try to treat everybody right. Even the one doing you wrong. Keep it in the hands of God and go on. I don't care anything about style. Want to look beautiful? Serve God. Addie Reeves was a beautiful woman.

— Tom Barton, *Savannah Morning News*

And as always, back for food and fellowship with Ms. Debra Selman leading the way. You have to keep the social in social change.

Eulogy for Mr. Welcome

— Tom Kohler

Waddie Welcome was all the things you see on your program. But Waddie Welcome was also a kidnapper. He had a way of catching your eye with his eyes, those fierce, intense eyes, and once he had you with his eyes, he would use that amazing smile, that quick laugh, to hold you.

Mr. Welcome captured Mrs. Addie Reeves many, many, years ago, and they have been a team for over 50 years. Mr. Welcome kidnapped me in a nursing home. That is where I first met him. I took Lester Johnson to meet him, and he kidnapped Lester. And then he grabbed Debra Selman and Jeff Alden and Susan Earl. He captured Susan's daughter, Emily. He captured my whole family, he captured Lester's office staff. He captured Sandy Mole and Wayne Daughtry and showed them that you didn't have to stay captured in a nursing home.

Mr. Welcome had a way of capturing people and not letting go until you were a little better person. And Lord, if Mr. Welcome didn't manage to capture you and turn you into a better person, his teammate Mrs. Reeves would. You know how she works: first it's, "Have a biscuit." Then it's, "How about some stewed chicken and dumplings?" And then it's, "Do unto others as you would have them do unto you," and you realize that the lady saying it is living it as well. Mrs. Reeves captured Jane Fishman and Linda Wittish, and bunches of others. Yes, Mr. Welcome was all those things that are listed on the program, but he was a kidnapper, too.

Here's a little story about how he grabbed two people from Cleveland, Ohio, and let them go as better people

On July 19, 1997, the video "Waddie Welcome: A Man Who Cannot be Denied" premiered at the Ralph Mark Gilbert Civil Rights Museum on MLK Jr. Boulevard. The museum itself had been recently completed thanks to the talents of the local art college, the brute determination of Mr. W.W. Law and the help of many, many local citizens. It is a place of power.

It was a hot Saturday night, and we had rented the museum and set up for 75 guests. 150 people came. We split the group, screened the video twice, managed to get an overflow crowd up and down the stairs and the elevator for the film and a reception in the historic four-story building. It was an exciting, intense two hours. Many of Mr. Welcome's family and church members had come, as well as several people from Atlanta. The *Savannah Morning News* covered the story.

As the evening wound down, a lovely young African-American couple came into the small front lobby of the museum. They were from Cleveland, in town as tourists, and seeing the museum bustling with people had assumed it was open.

They stepped in and took a moment to get their bearings in the room, taking in the mixture of black, white, young, old, standing, wheeling and reclining people. I heard the young woman ask a museum staff person, "What's going on here?" The staff person replied, "We are here to honor Mr. Welcome," as she nodded in his direction. The young woman's face went first to puzzled, then to reflective, and then to a soft smile with moist eyes. She had, I believe, just glimpsed a world better than the one she had stepped out of – or would be stepping back into – and she knew it.

And, that, my friends was, is, will always be, the power of this man named Waddie Welcome. At first he is a puzzlement to most people. Then to many people he brings reflection and insight and to some, a great and growing number around the world really, he brings hope. Hope of a better world, a world where there is more listening, more laughter, and more love. Mr. Welcome brought all three of these things – more listening, more laughter, more love – to life in his life. And the congregation says, AMEN!

Mrs. Reeves' Phone Book

— Tom Kohler

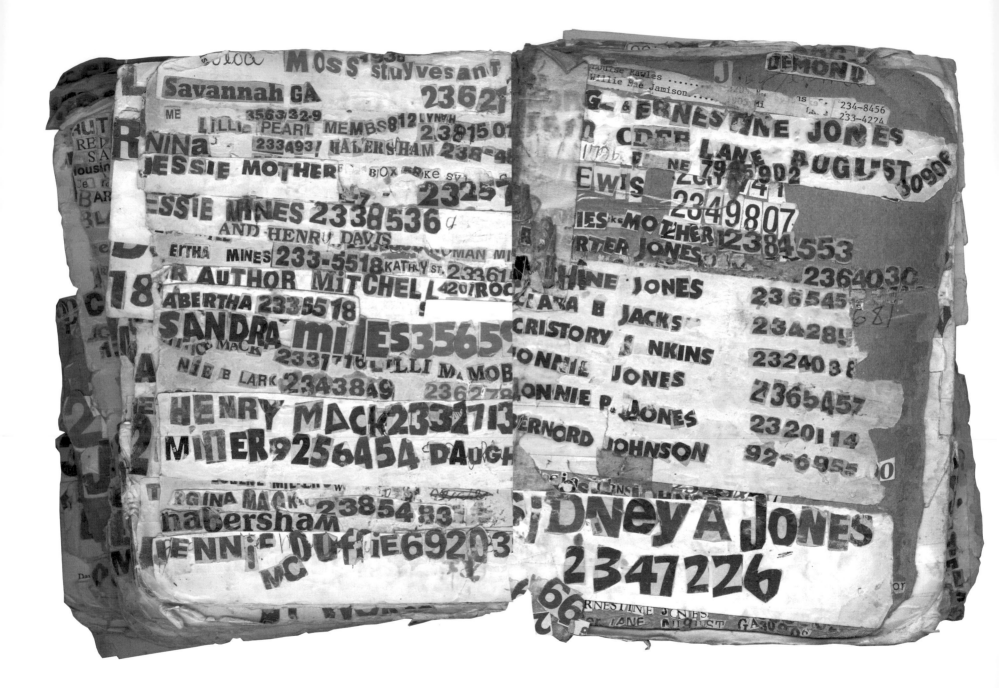

Visiting Mrs. Addie Reeves in her small apartment was a treat. She cooked almost non-stop and used only a small fan to beat back Savannah's hot and humid summers because "air conditioning makes you sick." Gospel music or a game show "for the noise" would be on. She would always be sitting in a gray metal rolling office chair, usually facing the front door — open in the spring, summer and fall — with her back to the doorway between living room and kitchen. Her walking cane would most often be leaned up next to her.

Her Bible was always in plain sight, most often in her lap. Her phone book, hand-made over, I'm guessing, at least a 25-year period would be on the couch or coffee table. Most pages were shirt cardboard, and all of the pages were filled with names and numbers of people. People Mrs. Reeves knew at church, people she knew as neighbors, people she had nursed back to health through her mission group. People, people, people. Each name was spelled letter by separate letter, cut out from a magazine or maybe the newspaper. Mrs. Reeves spent some time each day cutting letters out of magazines and storing them in a shallow cardboard box that she had sectioned into 36 little compartments by sewing cardboard strips into the box as dividers. Thousands of hand-cut little letters and numerals lay in this box each day. Each letter was taped or glued into the book to spell page after page of names. The book itself was bound with scotch tape, duct tape and glue. It was her phone book, hand-made a little each day as she met and pulled another person into her world.

I spent more and more time with Mrs. Reeves when she joined and served on the Chatham-Savannah Citizen Advocacy board – for three years, then six. And then, with a dispensation that defied the by-laws, she became our first and only eternal board member.

I always loved her phone book and when I took people over to meet Mrs. Reeves, I would ask her to let me show them the book. She would.

One day, she was probably 97 or 98 at the time, she told me, "Mr. Kohler, I'm gonna leave you my book." I told her that she was going to be coming to my funeral but I appreciated it. In her 99th year, the conversation turned a little more serious, but after her death, at 100 years and 30 days, I was still surprised and honored when her son, Robert, down from Chicago, told me that his mama had said for me to get the book. Her direction — "at my death this book goes to Mr. **Tom Kolah**" — had been cut and taped into the book, letter by letter in several places. I also have and treasure her Bible.

contemplation
and reflection

* What does Mr. Welcome teach us about hope?

* What valued social roles did Mr. Welcome play in his lifetime? How did each emerge? How were they strengthened?

* How are different people's gifts and talents expressed throughout the story?

* What examples do you see of protection? Advocacy? Community building?

The authors are available for contemplation and reflection with religious, civic, fraternal, business, family and other groups of citizens.

Tom Kohler
517 East Congress Street
Savannah, Georgia 31401
912-236-5798
tomkohler@bellsouth.net

Please go to www.waddiewelcome.com to order additional copies of the book. You will also find posters and postcards featuring Mrs. Reeves' phone book. All profits from the sale of these go to a trust fund for Mr. Welcome's great grand nephews pictured on page 70.

The video, "Waddie Welcome: A Man Who Cannot Be Denied," may be ordered from the Institute on Human Development and Disability, 850 College Station Road, Athens, GA 30602-4806. Cost: $89. Checks payable to IHDD.

about the authors

LYN BONHAM

Tom Kohler is and will be a life-long Savannahian. He is married to Betsy, and they have two enjoyable teenage daughters, Alice and Lucy. As coordinator of Chatham-Savannah Citizen Advocacy, he invites people into a variety of personal relationships with individual people whose lives are being diminished because of prejudice toward disability. Tom is active in a variety of formal and informal civic and other organizations and plays a leadership role in the Jim Collins Bar Alumni Association, the Savannah plant swap, Leadership Savannah and MOM (Men of Mind). He is a regular contributor to Letters to the Editor in the *Savannah Morning News*. Other interests include collecting and exhibiting local African-American advertising art, gardening and dancing to rock and roll.

LYN BONHAM

Born in New York City, **Susan Earl** is a Savannahian by choice. She is married to John, and their daughter, Emily, attends the Savannah College of Art and Design. Since 1980, in work with the Georgia Infirmary and as manager of St. Joseph's/Candler's SOURCE, she has enjoyed being able to connect people who are elderly or disabled with community supports. She is a past or present member of: 20/20-New York Woman Photographers, The Ossabaw Island Project, The Storytellers, Midtown Supper Club and the Chatham-Savannah Citizen Advocacy program committee. She has exhibited her photographs in galleries around the country and likes photographing people, listening to John Coltrane and walking in Forsyth Park. She has been a citizen advocate since 1989.

INCLUSION PRESS RESOURCE COLLECTION

47 Indian Trail, Toronto, ON Canada M6R 1Z8
Tel: 416-658-5363 Fax: 416-658-5067
e: inclusionpress@inclusion.com
WEB: www.inclusion.com

NEW Special Prices - Inclusion SPECIAL PACKS

Power of Three Pack - ABCD book + new PATH & MAPS Handbook + Make a Difference book
The Facilitation Pack - Facilitation for Inclusion DVD (new) + (new) PATH & MAPS Handbook
The ABCD PACK - ABCD in Action DVD + When People Care Enough to Act book
The Make a Difference PACK - Leader's Manual + MAD Guidebook +10 Learning Journey Booklets + Poster
The Community PACK - Members of Each Other & Celebrating the Ordinary - 2 books - J O'Brien & C O'Brien
The Education Book PACK - Inclusion: Recent Research & Inclusion: How To - 2 Books - Gary Bunch
Judith Snow Book PACK - Who's Drawing the Lines?; plus Now in One Book -(2 Books in one)
It's Your LIfe PACK - Neighbours Inc - 3 books - Living Your Own Life; Your Budget; Your Personal Assistants
Person Centered Planning PACK - A Little Book on Person Centered Planning + Voices of Experience
The Belonging Collection: Disability & Inclusion -PlayFair Kit + Choosing Our Future (Jean Vanier/L'Arche)
Inclusion Classics Book PACK [Action for Inclusion + Inclusion Papers]
Inclusion Classics DVD PACK (DVD) - [With a Little Help from My Friends + Kids Belong Together]
PATH in ACTION PACK (DVD) - 2 PATH Training "Videos" [PATH in Action + PATH Training + PATH Workbook]
PlayFair Teams Kit - (Teacher's book, Advocate's book , Intro CD, 2 posters)
When Spider Webs Unite PACK - Shafik Asante - Book and DVD
Golden Reflections PACK - Mike Yale - Book and audio MP3
Valued Experiences & Person Centered Direct Support Fold-out Posters (in Bundles)
Waddie Welcome Pack - the book and the DVD

BOOKS

ABCD:When People Care Enough to Act - ABCD in Action - Mike.Green
Action for Inclusion - Classic on Inclusion
All My Life's a Circle Expanded Edition- Circles, MAPS & PATH
The BIG Plan - A Good Life After School - Coulson & Simmons
Celebrating the Ordinary   John O'Brien, Connie Lyle O'Brien & Gail Jacob
Circle of Friends   by Bob & Martha Perske
Circles of Adults - Colin Newton & Derek Wilson (UK)
Community Lost & Found   Arthur Lockhart & Michael Clarke
The Community Place: Kate Foran with B. Jackson, P. Beeman, G. Ducharme   Ebook Version: $15.00
Conversations on Citizenship & Person-Centered Planning - O'Brien & Blessing
Creating Circles of Friends - Colin Newton & Derek Wilson (UK)
Directory of Disability Organizations in Canada (2007-08 edition)
Do You Hear What I Hear? - Janice Fialka & Karen Mikus
Dream Catchers & Dolphins   Marsha Forest and Jack Pearpoint
Each Belongs - Jim Hansen with Leyden, Bunch, Pearpoint (book with CD)
Equity, Social Justice and Disability in Schools - Gary Bunch et al
Finding Meaning in the Work - (CD + Manual/Curriculum) (O'Briens)
Free to Fly - A Story of Manic Depression   Caroline Fei-Yeng Kwok
Friends & Inclusion: Five Approaches to Building Relationships: P. Hutchison; J. Lord, K. Lord
From Behind the Piano - by Jack Pearpoint & What's Really Worth Doing by Judith Snow
   - Now in One Book (printed together)

Golden Reflections   - Mike Yale (also available as an MP3 - also $25)
Hints for Graphic Facilitators   - Jack Pearpoint
The Inclusion Papers - Strategies & Stories - Forest & Pearpoint editors
Inclusion: How To   Essential Classroom Strategies - Gary Bunch
Inclusive Education: Emergent Solutions   G. Bunch & A. Valeo
Incurably Human   Micheline Mason
A Little Book About Person Centered Planning
        John O'Brien & Connie Lyle O'Brien with Forest, Lovett, Mount, Pearpoint, Small, Snow, and Strully
Make a Difference: Direct Support Guidebook (J. O'Brien & B. Mount)
Make a Difference: Leader's Resource Kit (Instructor's book + CD)
Make a Difference: Learning Journey Booklet (Packet of 10)
MAPS & PATH: A Workbook for Facilitators   John O'Brien & Jack Pearpoint - New Edition 2007
Members of Each Other   John O'Brien & Connie Lyle O'Brien
One Candle Power - Cathy Ludlum & Communitas
PATH & MAPS Handbook: Person-Centered Ways to Build Community (NEW)
PATH Workbook - 2nd Edition Planning Positive Possible Futures
Perske - Pencil Portraits 1971-1990
Planning for a Real Life After School: School Transition
Planning for a Real Life After School: School Transition: Plain Language Edition
PlayFair Teams: A Community Advocate's Manual
The Poetry of David Moreau: If You're Happy & You Know It Clap Your Hand
Remembering the Soul of Our Work   John OBrien & Connie Lyle-O'Brien
Restorative Justice Art Lockhart, Lynn Zammit, Randy Charboneau
Seeing the Charade - Carole Tashie and Team
Still Determined After All These Tears: Regina Louise DeMarasse
        Ebook Version: $15.00   Audio Book CD's (16): $60.00
Supporting Learners with Intellectual Challenge Gary Bunch
Voices of Experience: Implementing Person-Centered Planning
        Editors: John O'Brien & Connie Lyle O'Brien
Waddie Welcome & the Beloved Community   Tom Kohler & Susan Earl
When Spider Webs Unite Community & Inclusion - Shafik Asante
Who's Drawing the Lines? - Judith Snow
Yes! She Knows She's Here Nicola Schaefer's Book about Kathrine
Inclusion – Exclusion Poster (18 X 24)
Person Centered Direct Support Foldout (call for bulk rates)

MEDIA: DVDs • CD-ROMs

ABCD in ACTION - DVD-Mike Green, Henry Moore & John McKnight
Doing Our Best Work: 10 Ingredients of Quality Support - Peter Leidy - DVD
EVERYONE Has a GIFT   J McKnight - Building Communities of Capacity - (DVD)

Facilitation for Inclusion with PATH & MAPS - New training DVD
Finding Meaning in the Work (CD + Curriculum) - J O'Brien & C Lyle O'Brien
Friendship DVD   Judith Snow, Marsha Forest & Jack Pearpoint on Friendship
The Inclusion Classics - 2 classic inclusion videos on DVD
Make a Difference: Leader's Resource Kit (Instructor's book + CD)
The MAPS Collection - DVD (2 MAPS Training videos on DVD)
My Life, My Choice - DVD   (7 stories of adults with full lives)
The PATH Collection - DVD (2 PATH Training videos on DVD)
PATH Demo Video   Univ of Dayton Ohio - DVD of Workshop on PATH

PATH in ACTION   Working with Groups -Training DVD for Path with Groups
PATH TRAINING DVD   Intro Training DVD - An Individual Path {Joe's Path}
Person Centered Direct Support - CD - 4 minute video & powerpoint
PlayFair Teams CD-ROM   An introduction to PlayFair Teams
ReDiscovering MAPS Charting Your Journey - MAPS training (DVD)
Seven Ways to Prevent a Crisis - Peter Leidy - DVD
TOOLS for CHANGE - The CD-Rom for Person Centred Planning
Waddie Welcome: A Man Who Could Not Be Denied - DVD
When Spider Webs Unite - DVD - Shafik Asante in Action

new DVD   **Mindfulness**   **CD: Tools for Change Tools for Person Centered Planning**

*Join us at the **Toronto Summer Institute***
July in Toronto
Inclusion • Community • Diversity
www.inclusion.com

Training Events:
Made to measure!
PATH & Maps; Make a Difference
Contact: inclusionpress@inclusion.com

Credit Cards on the Net (secure), Cheques, Money Orders, Purchase Orders
• Prices subject to change without notice.
Shipping prices for North America only.
Elsewhere by quote.
• Shipping: Books: $10 for 1st + $3/copy;
Packs: $15 for 1st+ $4/copy.
OR, On bulk orders: 15% of total order cost
- which ever is less.

Newer Resources

• **Conversations on Citizenship & Person-Centered Planning** - New
• **Who's Drawing the Lines?** - Judith Snow - new
• **Equity, Social Justice and Disability in Schools** - Gary Bunch et al - new
• **Facilitation for Inclusion with PATH & MAPS** - New training DVD
• **PATH & MAPS Handbook: Person-Centered Ways to Build Community** (NEW)
• **Power of Three Pack** - ABCD book + new PATH & MAPS Handbook + Make a Difference book
• **It's Your LIfe PACK** - Neighbours Inc
• **Belonging Collection:** Disability & Inclusion
• Gentle Heart Fearless Mind: Mindfulness DVD + Booklet: Alan Sloan (NEW)
• **Friends & Inclusion:** Five Approaches to Building Relationships: P. Hutchison; J. Lord, K. Lord (NEW)
• Make a Difference Pack: Leader's Manual + MAD Guidebook +10 Learning Journey Booklets
• **PATH & MAPS Handbook:** Person-Centered Ways to Build Community (NEW)
• **Make a Difference Pack:** Leader's Manual + MAD Guidebook +10 Learning Journey Booklets
• Golden Reflections: - written by Vargus Yale (Mike's seeing-eye guide dog) with Mike Yale
         Also available in Audio MP3 read by Don Herron and as a package with the book
• Inclusive Education: Emergent Solutions   Gary Bunch & Angela Valeo
• Planning for a Real Life After School: Transition from School (2 editions)
• The Poetry of David Moreau: If You're Happy and You Know It Clap Your Hand
• Doing Our Best Work: 10 Ingredients of Quality Support: Peter Leidy - DVD
• ABCD in Action - DVD & Book -When People Care Enough to Act
• My Life My Choice - DVD - Seven Adults living full lives in the community
• Make a Difference - book; Leaders Guide, Work Booklets
• The Big Plan - A Good Life After School - Transition Planning with groups
• Each Belongs - book & CD - The 1st Inclusive School Board ever!
• PlayFair Teams - 2 books, DVD + Posters - blended teams in schools.
• Find Meaning in the Work - CD & Manual/Curriculum - presentation ready!

Name: _____
Organization:_____
Address:_____
City: _____
Prov/State _____ Post Code/ZIP _____
Wk Phone _____ Cheque Enclosed _____
Hm Phone _____ Fax _____
E-Mail _____ Web Page:_____